A Time Line of the American Revolution

Lynn George

The Rosen Publishing Group's
READING ROOM

New York

Published in 2003 by The Rosen Publishing Group, Inc.
29 East 21st Street, New York, NY 10010

Copyright © 2003 by The Rosen Publishing Group, Inc.

First Library Edition 2003

All rights reserved. No part of this book may be reproduced in any form without permission in writing from the publisher, except by a reviewer.

Book Design: Michael Flynn

Photo Credits: Cover (background), p. 1 (background) © Grant V. Faint/The Image Bank; cover (Boston Massacre, Boston Tea Party), pp. 1 (Boston Massacre, Boston Tea Party), 9, 11, 12 © North Wind Pictures; cover (Patrick Henry), pp. 1 (Patrick Henry), 6-7, 13, 17, 20-21 (background) © Bettman/Corbis; cover (Signing of Declaration of Independence), pp. 1 (Signing of Declaration of Independence), 14-15 © Francis G. Mayer/Corbis; p. 5 © Photo World/FPG International; p. 16 © Leonard de Selva/Corbis; p. 19 © Library of Congress, Washington, D.C./SuperStock; p. 20 (U.S. Constitution) © Joseph Sohm, ChromoSohm Inc./Corbis; pp. 2-24 (paper texture) © creativ collection.

Library of Congress Cataloging-in-Publication Data

George, Lynn.
  A time line of the American Revolution / Lynn George.
    p. cm. — (The Rosen Publishing Group's reading room collection)
Summary: A discussion of the American Revolution which takes a chronological approach, focusing on the development and use of a time line.
  ISBN 978-1-4358-8953-8
  1. United States—History—Revolution,
1775-1783—Chronology—Juvenile literature. 2. United
States—History—Colonial period, ca.
1600-1775—Chronology—Juvenile literature. [1. United
States—History—Revolution, 1775-1783—Chronology. 2. United
States—History—Colonial period, ca. 1600-1775—Chronology.] I.
Title. II. Series.
  E209 .G46 2003
  973.3'02'02—dc21

2001008066

Manufactured in the United States of America

For More Information
The American Revolution for Kids
http://artemis.simmons.edu/~williamf/AmRev/index.html

Liberty! Chronicle of the Revolution (PBS)
http://www.pbs.org/ktca/liberty/chronicle/timeline.html

Contents

What Is a Time Line?	4
The English Colonies in America	6
The Colonies Grow	8
England Taxes the Colonies	10
The Colonies Fight Back	12
The Protests Lead to War	14
The Early Years of the Revolutionary War	16
The Colonies Win Their Freedom	18
Creating a New Government	20
Using Time Lines	22
Glossary	23
Index	24

What Is a Time Line?

Many people make time lines to study history. A time line shows important **events** and the dates those events happened. It shows the events in order, starting with the earliest and ending with the latest. A time line does not give all of the information about each event, only the basic facts. It is a good way to get a quick idea of what happened during a certain period of time and how all the events fit together.

A time line is a good way to study the life of a famous person from history. Here, we see important events in the life of George Washington, one of the great leaders of the American Revolution.

1732	George Washington is born in the colony of Virginia.
1755	Washington becomes commander of Virginia's soldiers in French and Indian War.
1774	Washington is elected to First Continental Congress.
1775	Washington is elected to Second Continental Congress. The Congress chooses Washington as commander in chief of the Continental army.
1787	Washington is elected to lead the meeting to write the Constitution.
1789	Washington is elected as first president of the United States.

George Washington

The English Colonies in America

A time line can help us understand how the English **colonies** became the United States. We can begin by looking at the time line to find out when the colonies were started. The first successful English colony was started in Virginia in 1607. By 1733, there were thirteen English colonies. Look at the time line to find the names of the colonies and the dates they were **founded**.

How many years did it take to establish all thirteen colonies? Subtract 1607 from 1733 to get your answer.

- **1607** Colony of Virginia founded.
- **1620s** Massachusetts, New Hampshire, and New York founded.
- **1630s** Connecticut, Maryland, Rhode Island, and Delaware founded.
- **1643** Pennsylvania founded.
- **1653** North Carolina founded.
- **1660** New Jersey founded.
- **1670** South Carolina founded.
- **1733** Georgia founded.

The Colonies Grow

In England, news of the colonies' success spread. As people heard about the freedom the colonists had in America, more of them wanted to come to the colonies. The population of the colonies grew as more people came to America.

Use the time line to find the total population in 1753. You can do this by adding 250,000 and 1,083,000. The answer is 1,333,000. What was the total population in 1775? Add 1,333,000 to 1,167,000 to get your answer.

- **1700** Population of colonies is 250,000.

- **1753** Population of colonies has grown by 1,083,000.

- **1775** Population of colonies has grown by another 1,167,000.

England Taxes the Colonies

In 1754, the French attacked American colonies to get more land. The colonists helped the English fight the French in the French and Indian War. England won, but the war had cost a lot of money. England put soldiers in the colonies to prevent another war, but could not afford to pay them. England **taxed** the colonies to make money.

How many years passed between the beginning of the French and Indian War and the time England passed the Stamp Act?

- **1754** French and Indian War begins. England fights France for control of American colonies.
- **1763** England wins French and Indian War.
- **1764** England passes Currency Act. Colonies can no longer put out their own money. England makes and controls all money. England passes Sugar Act. Taxes are put on imported sugar, cloth, coffee, and other things.
- **1765** England passes Stamp Act. Colonists must pay a tax every time they buy something printed on paper.

French and Indian War

The Colonies Fight Back

Many colonists were angry about the taxes England had placed on them. Colonial leaders and governments joined groups of colonists to **protest** the taxes. England continued to tax the colonies.

Look at the time line to find out which of these happened first: the Boston **Massacre**, Patrick Henry's speech, or the Townshend Acts. How many years after the Sons of Liberty was formed did England **repeal** the Townshend Acts?

Boston Massacre

1765 Group in Boston forms Sons of Liberty to protest Stamp Act. Sons of Liberty soon spreads throughout colonies. Patrick Henry makes speech against Stamp Act to Virginia leaders. Virginia government protests Stamp Act. Leaders of colonies meet to protest Stamp Act.

1766 England repeals Stamp Act.

1767 England passes Townshend Acts, which tax tea, paper, glass, and other things.

1770 Boston Massacre. English soldiers shoot at crowd of angry colonists, killing five. England repeals Townshend Acts except for tax on tea.

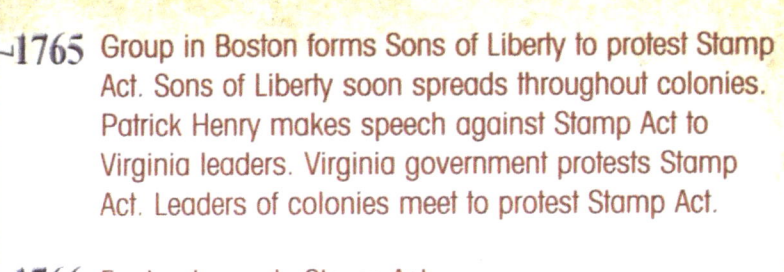

Patrick Henry

The Protests Lead to War

Soon the colonists were at war with England. The Continental Congress met in Philadelphia, Pennsylvania, to **declare** the colonies' freedom from England.

Use this time line and the time line on page 13 to find out how the colonists protested the Townshend Acts. What were the protests and when did they happen? How many years after the Townshend Acts were passed did the Battles of Lexington and Concord happen?

Signing of the Declaration of Independence

1773 Tea Act allows England to sell tea to the colonists for less than the price of tea from other countries. England hopes this will make colonists buy English tea and pay the tax on it. Angry colonists protest with the Boston Tea Party, dumping tea into Boston Harbor.

1774 England passes the Intolerable Acts. The Acts close Boston Harbor until colonists pay for the destroyed tea. First Continental Congress meets to prepare a protest against England.

1775 Patrick Henry makes speech protesting the Intolerable Acts. Paul Revere makes his famous ride to warn the people in Concord, Massachusetts, that English soldiers are coming. Colonial soldiers fight English soldiers at Lexington and Concord. These are the first battles of the American Revolution. The Second Continental Congress meets. They create the Continental army and make George Washington the leader.

1776 Second Continental Congress writes and approves the Declaration of Independence.

The Early Years of the Revolutionary War

At first the colonies lost many battles and won only a few. They might not have been able to continue the war without the help they received from France. For how many years did France give secret help to the colonies before they sent soldiers?

Look at the time line to find out which of these events happened after the battle at Princeton: English soldiers captured New York City, Lafayette joined Washington's soldiers, or English soldiers chased Washington's men out of New Jersey.

Lafayette

1776 English soldiers capture New York City from Washington's soldiers. English soldiers chase Washington's soldiers out of New Jersey. Washington's soldiers win a battle at Trenton, New Jersey, and capture many English soldiers. France secretly gives money and guns to colonists.

1777 Washington's soldiers win a battle at Princeton, New Jersey. Washington's army goes to Valley Forge, Pennsylvania, for the winter. During the winter, many soldiers die from cold, sickness, and lack of food.

1778 A French soldier named Lafayette joins Washington's soldiers and works without pay. France officially joins the war and sends soldiers to help the colonies.

Washington and Lafayette at Valley Forge

The Colonies Win Their Freedom

The colonies finally won the war. The last big battle happened in 1781. After two more years of fighting, the colonies and England signed a **treaty** that said the colonies were a free country—the United States of America.

How many years after the Revolutionary War began was the Treaty of Paris signed? You can look at the time line on page 15 to find out when the first battle of the war happened.

1780 Francis Marion, the "Swamp Fox," and a small band of soldiers attack English soldiers in South Carolina. They hide from the English in swamps.

1781 Colonial and French soldiers win a big battle at Yorktown, Virginia, and capture 8,000 English soldiers. British General Cornwallis surrenders.

1782 English and colonial leaders meet in Paris, France, to begin peace talks. They write the Treaty of Paris.

1783 Congress approves the Treaty of Paris. Leaders of England and the colonies sign the treaty. The last English soldiers leave the United States.

Cornwallis Surrenders to Washington at Yorktown, Virginia

Creating a New Government

The new country had to create a new government for itself. A system of rules called the **Articles of Confederation** set up the first national government. After a few years, leaders wrote the **Constitution** to create a better government. The Constitution became law after nine states approved it. Look at the time line to find out when that happened. How many years later was the **Bill of Rights** added to the Constitution?

United States Constitution

1781 Articles of Confederation are written.

1787 Leaders write new Constitution. Delaware, Pennsylvania, and New Jersey approve Constitution.

1788 Georgia, Connecticut, Massachusetts, Maryland, South Carolina, New Hampshire, Virginia, and New York approve Constitution.

1789 North Carolina approves Constitution. Washington becomes first president. Members of Congress are chosen by the states. New York City is made the capital of the United States.

1790 Rhode Island approves Constitution. Capital moves to Philadelphia.

1791 Bill of Rights is added to Constitution. It lists rights that the government cannot take away from the people. Washington chooses permanent site for new capital to be built. It is named Washington, D.C., in his honor.

Using Time Lines

Time lines help us see how one event caused later events. For example, we can follow events from the French and Indian War to the American Revolution. Basic math skills can help us understand the facts on a time line, or how much time passed between important events. When we see that it took 126 years to found the first thirteen colonies, we can conclude that it was hard at first to get people to come to America. When we see that the colonists' protests caused England to repeal the Stamp Act after only a year, we can conclude that the protests were angry and forceful. What other things have you learned from the time lines in this book?

Glossary

Articles of Confederation	The first set of rules for the government of the United States.
Bill of Rights	The first ten statements added to the Constitution, which list rights the government cannot take away from the people.
colony	Land that has been settled by people who live in one country but are ruled by another.
constitution	A system of rules for a country that tells the powers and duties of the government and the rights of the people.
declare	To make something known officially.
event	Something important that happens.
found	To set up. To establish.
massacre	The act of killing helpless people.
protest	To object strongly to something.
repeal	To put an official end to a law.
tax	To make people pay money to support the government.
treaty	An agreement between two countries.

Index

A
Articles of Confederation, 20, 21

B
Battles of Lexington and Concord, 14, 15
Bill of Rights, 20, 21
Boston Massacre, 12, 13
Boston Tea Party, 15

C
colonists, 8, 10, 12, 13, 14, 15, 17, 22
colony(ies), 5, 6, 7, 8, 10, 12, 13, 14, 16, 17, 18, 22
Constitution, 5, 20, 21
Continental Congress, 5, 14, 15
Cornwallis, General, 18
Currency Act, 10

D
Declaration of Independence, 15

E
England, 8, 10, 12, 13, 14, 15, 18, 22
English, 6, 10, 13, 15, 16, 17, 18

F
France, 10, 16, 17, 18
French and Indian War, 5, 10, 22

H
Henry, Patrick, 12, 13, 15

I
Intolerable Acts, 15

L
Lafayette, 16, 17

M
Marion, Francis, 18

P
Philadelphia, 14, 21

R
Revere, Paul, 15

S
Sons of Liberty, 12, 13
Stamp Act, 10, 13, 22
Sugar Act, 10

T
Tea Act, 15
Townshend Acts, 12, 13, 14
Treaty of Paris, 18

U
United States, 5, 6, 18, 21

V
Valley Forge, 17
Virginia, 5, 6, 7, 13, 18, 21

W
Washington, George, 5, 15, 16, 17, 21
Washington, D.C., 21

www.ingramcontent.com/pod-product-compliance
Lightning Source LLC
Chambersburg PA
CBHW041220070526
44584CB00001B/32